DETERRENCE

By Lord Loveday Ememe and available from Lulu
The constitution and policing
Heresy
Starfleet
The Supernatural
Creation

www.lulu.com

Copyright© Lord Loveday Ememe 2012.

The author asserts the moral right to be recognized as the author of this work.

ISBN: 978-1-4716-4799-4

Table of Contents

1. CRIMINALITY

It is important to be clear about what the constitution, which is the Christian principles, civil rights considers to be crimes, criminal behaviour or activity. This should not be confused with the demonic practices of the uncivilized with regard to their delusional creation of crimes associated with the conditions resulting from the misuse of their supernatural powers and senses. Crimes, according to the constitution can only be committed by the uncivilized because they have supernatural powers and senses. It is impossible for the civilized to commit crimes because of the lack of supernatural powers and senses.

The constitution defines a crime as the misuse of supernatural powers and senses to harm the civilized mentally or physically or to breach the peace in a civilized society.

Contrary to the guidance of the constitution, the uncivilized have misused their supernatural powers and senses to create living conditions to make life impossible for those different from them, including making life impossible for the civilized.

Contrary to the guidance of the constitution, the uncivilized are pretending to be of the civilized nature because of the moral superiority of the civilized while everything is falling apart, neglecting their duties and obstructing the constitutional authority of the civilized. It is unlawful for the uncivilized to pretend to be civilized with the intention of denying the civilized the constitutional right, civil right, to govern. The civilized are naturally commissioners of police with the civil right of dominion over this planet. It is unlawful for the uncivilized to impersonate law enforcement officers, the civilized, with the intention of denying the civilized the constitutional authority meant for the civilized to establish and maintain law and order.

There is a difference between the uncivilized pretending to be civilized contrary to the guidance of the constitution with the intention to misuse their supernatural powers and senses to harm the civilized mentally or physically or to breach the peace in a civilized society and the uncivilized pretending to be civilized to aspire to the qualities or characteristics of the civilized for the purpose of maintaining law and order.

According to the guidance of the constitution, the Christian principles, civil rights, the civilized are confirmed as morally superior to the uncivilized. The uncivilized have been doing everything possible to undermine or challenge the moral superiority of the civilized contrary to the guidance of the constitution. They are behaving like rebels without a cause. It is similar to sibling rivalry with the added effect of creating hell on earth contrary to the instructions of the constitution. According to the guidance of the constitution, it is unlawful for the uncivilized to misuse their supernatural powers and senses to alter the natural life span of the civilized, with the unlawful introduction of death, illness, ageing, regardless of their personal views on life.

The uncivilized have unlawfully introduced illnesses into the lives of the civilized by giving names or medical terms to the misuse of their supernatural powers and senses, as if that is meant to give legitimacy to the sadism of the uncivilized when they misuse their supernatural powers and senses to harm the civilized mentally or physically.

According to the guidance of the constitution, given the differences in the natures of the civilized and uncivilized, the purpose of the law or a constitution, is similar to the principles of the imposition of martial law, to regulate the use of supernatural powers and senses because of the on-going threat and continuous existence of supernatural powers and senses. The civilized are representations of the law in living form. The law commissions a legitimate police force to establish and maintain peace and security. This makes the civilized that are representations of the law in living form commissioners of police. This is a role that the uncivilized are not naturally qualified to assume. This requirement of the constitution for the civilized to be confirmed officially as commissioners of police provides the intended personal security for the civilized and provides peace and security in a civilized society.

This means that the civilized are automatically entitled to the uniforms and salary of a commissioner of the metropolitan police force. The obvious reluctance of the uncivilized to obey the instructions of the constitution with regard to the imposition of martial law is because they feel threatened by it. If they feel threatened by the law, how do they think the civilized feel about their supernatural powers and senses? Given the magnitude of the misuse of the supernatural powers and senses of the uncivilized to continuously harm the civilized mentally and physically and to breach the peace in a civilized society, the guidance of the constitution on the imposition of martial law is completely correct. The uncivilized can look at the uniforms and salary of a commissioner of police as part of the constitution or nature of the civilized; in the same way they consider their supernatural powers and senses to be part of their constitution or nature. This will help them better understand the constitutional authority of the civilized. This entitlement applies regardless of age. For the uncivilized to try to obstruct access to these natural entitlements, is not different from trying to unlawfully kill the civilized. The current salary of a commissioner of the metropolitan police force is about £260,000 a year. According to the guidance of the constitution, to deny the civilized our civil rights (administrative powers or the right of dominion over the planet), is to make the civilized incomplete, which is not different from being dead. This conspiracy by the uncivilized is unlawful.

As a consequence of the delusional way the uncivilized live their lives, they are in denial about their extremely hostile nature, which has compromised their ability to comprehend, coupled with the limitations of their supernatural instincts. This is part of the reason they plan the lives of the civilized to revolve around having unnecessary dangerous contact with them outside the guidelines stipulated by the constitution.

They set out deliberately contrary to the guidelines of the constitution to compromise the education of the civilized, like the serpent in the Garden of Eden, to mislead the civilized whose source of knowledge is linked to trust and education, by misusing their supernatural powers and senses to make the civilized eat meat, fish, and eggs. They believed that these compromises will give them the moral authority to unlawfully use their supernatural powers and senses to alter the civil nature of the civilized, in order to undermine law and order. Because they are blinded by their supernatural instincts they failed to understand that the lesson about the Garden of Eden in the Christian teachings was an education about the impossibilities of compromising or altering the civil nature of the civilized. Also the problem with eating they encountered was that if you are meant to be a vegetarian you will not want to eat meat, fish or eggs unless there was a misuse of supernatural powers and senses. Why will you want to eat something you will not naturally want to eat?

According to the guidance of the constitution, it is a serious crime for the uncivilized to misuse their supernatural powers and senses to give false impressions that the civilized are capable of committing crimes, expressed or implied.

The uncivilized live their lives delusively, they pretend to be civilized and believe that they are of the civilized nature when they are not, as a consequence they cannot comprehend the reasoning or purpose of civil rights for the civilized and its relevance in establishing peace and security for the civilized and in a civilized society. Because of the delusional way they live their lives, pretending to be civilized; they take for granted the importance of civil rights in particular the civil right of dominion to the civilized. They have arrived at the conclusion that the civilized do not need these civil powers that form part of our constitution. If they can do without it why can the civilized not do without it? This is the reasoning of the uncivilized as a result of pretending to be civilized. They cannot comprehend that these civil powers, the right of dominion over the planet is incorporated into the civil nature of the civilized. The supernatural instincts of the uncivilized cannot allow them to comprehend that these civil powers are part of the civil nature of the civilized and protects the independence of the civilized from the intrusive nature of the uncivilized.

The uncivilized collectively should be known as or their new name should be set up or framed, because of how they misuse their supernatural powers and senses to create conditions illegally to give false impressions that the civilized are capable of sinning or committing crimes. It is enough for them to establish culpability, which they then believe gives them the legitimacy to misuse their supernatural powers and senses under the guise of retaliation or punishment to harm the civilized mentally or physically. The constitution has correctly established that the differences in the natures of the civilized and the uncivilized mean that the civilized are incapable of committing crimes or sinning. The source of any problem or wrongdoing will be amongst the uncivilized and not the civilized. According to the guidance of the constitution, when the uncivilized illegally misuse their supernatural powers and senses to harm the civilized mentally or physically or to breach the peace in a civilized society, they become fugitives from real justice and cannot represent the interest of the civilized or speak for the civilized.

According to the guidance of the constitution, the uncivilized are not allowed to communicate to the civilized supernaturally in the manner found in the Christian teachings in the stories outside the Garden of Eden. The uncivilized are not allowed communicating to the civilized in riddles, it is an abuse of power to be deliberately vague or create puzzles for the civilized to solve before they are able to understand their rights or have access to our entitlements.

According to the guidance of the constitution, it is illegal for the uncivilized to have or initiate direct or indirect contact with the civilized without the official confirmation of the civilized as commissioners of the metropolitan police force with the rights and entitlements or privileges that come with it, in order to create the necessary balance for the personal security of the civilized and for the peace and security in a civilized society.

There are a lot of dramatics or shows with no substance with regard to the civil or administrative powers meant for the civilized by the uncivilized, this is because these administrative powers that are meant for the civilized are taken illegally by the uncivilized, it is a thrill for them to assume the role meant for the civilized which is not allowed or forbidden because of their uncivilized natures.

The effect of the misuse of supernatural powers and senses of one person on the civilized is very unhealthy, seriously traumatic psychologically, even more so when the uncivilized as a collective misuse their supernatural powers and senses to persecute the civilized as is currently the case.

The magnitude of the wickedness of the uncivilized as a collective evidenced from their on-going persecution of those different from them including the civilized is beyond what any reasonable person can comprehend.

The obvious weakness of the uncivilized that makes them easy prey for their enemies is their inability to comprehend when their actions have done irreparable damage to a relationship. Their judgements and actions are guided by their supernatural instincts. With this in mind they are a serious liability to the security of those different from them, and cannot reasonably expect to represent the interest of those different from them or to speak for them. Those different from them will want to avoid contact with the uncivilized because of their hostile nature and the attacks on them they will inevitably attract.

When the uncivilized get the civilized used to eating cooked food, it goes without saying that they are required by law to make available to the civilized the most convenient, hygienic way to access cooked food that will satisfy the conditions similar to those in the Garden of Eden, which is through replicator technology evidenced in science fiction films like Star Trek. It is a criminal offence for the uncivilized not to provide the most convenient way to access cooked food that does not require the civilized to have contact with the uncivilized.

The jokes, games and contacts of the uncivilized are too heavy-handed for the civilized, and are potentially extremely hostile, unhealthy for the civilized.

The uncivilized claim that their supernatural powers and senses make them morally superior to the civilized contrary to the guidance of the constitution. To reinforce this false claim, the uncivilized misuse their supernatural powers and senses to create horrific living conditions for the civilized to establish dependency which has the opposite effect of reinforcing the guidance of the constitution that the civilized are morally superior to the uncivilized.

The uncivilized need to be aware that they are always under caution, when in communication with the civilized, similar to the caution associated with the right to silence because of the effects of the misuse of their supernatural powers and senses on the civilized. The civilized are always in every situation in good faith, and do not welcome the misuse of supernatural powers and senses by the uncivilized.

There is a character in the television drama series Star Trek the next generation called Data, an Android, the ability or knowledge of the android is limited to how it has been programmed by its creator. Although the civilized are different because we have freewill or consciousness, and the civilized are naturally good, our development or knowledge is dependent on a different type of programming, education. The uncivilized deliberately interfered with our source of knowledge, a collective conspiracy by the uncivilized to compromise the only source of knowledge for the civilized and the education or programming of the civilized is corrupt. When the uncivilized deliberately conspire to compromise the development of the civilized, they try to judge the civilized, ignoring their deliberate conspiracy to corrupt the programming or education of the civilized.

According to the guidance of the constitution, the rights of the civilized confirm that the differences in the natures of the civilized and the uncivilized mean that the civilized were created with a specific purpose, to rule. The uncivilized are not allowed under any circumstances to obstruct the civil right of the civilized to govern. The position of the commissioner of the metropolitan police force in the United Kingdom fulfils this requirement for the civilized, with some minor adjustments. The adjustments are to apply the guidance of the constitution correctly, given the differences, confirming the position as the top government position in the United Kingdom. It is also possible to have more than one commissioner depending on how many civilized people are in the country. The position is honorary or symbolic, which guarantees the personal security of the civilized and at the same time provides peace and security in the country.

It is unlawful for the uncivilized to misuse their supernatural powers and senses to create serious problems like famines, diseases, things they refer to as natural disasters like earthquakes, thunder storms, flooding and car accidents, aeroplane accidents etc., in order to make the vulnerable including the civilized to live in constant fear. The uncivilized enjoy the fear they have programmed into the lives of the civilized because they feed off dependency and being worshipped by the civilized.

The uncivilized because they are guided by their supernatural instincts, they look at law and order matters as games to play. Because they are guided by the supernatural instincts they are unaware of the extremely disruptive, hostile nature of their actions. They behave like very young children that cannot comprehend the dangers to themselves and others of their actions. Their total disregard for the law evidenced by their abominable actions is because of their misguided superiority complex, which accounts for the seeds of lawlessness being sown with every misguided decision they make.

According to the guidance of the constitution, the Christian principles, civil rights, it is not a small matter for the uncivilized to be in the presence of the civilized, the uncivilized need to be well versed in civil rights law or protocols, intelligent or well mannered. I believe the history of the United Kingdom in particular England, is a lesson in etiquette, of how the commoners or the uncivilized are required to behave when in the presence of the nobles or the civilized. It was never allowed for the uncivilized or commoners to try to pretend or pass themselves off as nobles or the civilized.

The police forces in the United Kingdom operating illegally without the authorization of the civilized and operating outside the guidance of the constitution do not have a broad definition of crime that deliberately discriminates against the civilized that are recognized by the constitution as the only legitimate law enforcement officers or commissioners of police. This will suggest according to the guidance of the constitution that the police forces are composed of demons operating for the benefit of demons contrary to the guidance of the constitution. This is why they are accused of being institutionally racist; they are using the law for illegal purposes.

Only God can make the distinction of those amongst the uncivilized that are Angels or Demons, the civilized as representations of God and have the civil powers or natural instincts to make that distinction. As someone of a civilized nature, I cannot honestly identify any Angels amongst the uncivilized. It must be noted that physical appearance is not a determining factor in the identification of an Angel.

The comfort, rights and privileges of the civilized is taken extremely seriously by the constitution because the peace and security of the planet is linked to it. The uncivilized are not allowed under any circumstances to speak in riddles to the civilized regarding the official confirmation of the civilized as commissioners of police. The constitution is clear in its guidance that the uncivilized that misuse their supernatural powers and senses to harm the civilized mentally or physically cannot be allowed to get away with it. They are expected to be severely punished to avoid sowing the seeds of the continuous persecution of the civilized, even if the uncivilized try to disguise their attacks as jokes and games. The constitution does not recognize any relationships between the civilized and the uncivilized outside that already predetermined by the constitution.

As someone of a civilized nature I am constantly being bullied by the uncivilized with the misuse of their supernatural powers and senses into role plays specifically aimed at the persecution of the civilized and to undermine our constitutional authority. These forced role plays give false impressions that the uncivilized can rely on, to unlawfully misuse their supernatural powers and senses to try to compromise the civil nature of the civilized in order to undermine our civil rights. The uncivilized try to initiate unwanted contact with the civilized, to try to intimidate, humiliate the civilized by misusing their supernatural powers and senses. It is an ambitious objective to accomplish considering that life is naturally a humiliating experience for them. They only need to look at themselves to understand the impossibility of the plan. The discomfort experienced by the civilized with contact with the uncivilized is because of being repulsed by the barbarism of the uncivilized. The repulsion is worse than but similar in principle to the way people look at paedophiles.

The significance or importance of the word GOD in our lives which the civilized represent is about the law. And the law or civil rights originated in the Garden of Eden with Adam.

The uncivilized have introduced the practice of politics contrary to the guidance of the constitution. Politics implies that there is no constitution and directly challenges the viability, competence or sensibility of the constitution, which is blasphemy, treason. The practice of politics is a criminal activity, which persecutes the vulnerable including the civilized. It encourages discriminating against those different from you or who have different views or opinions from yours. It encourages the interference with the personal freedoms of those different from you or who have different opinions or views from yours. The practice of politics is a demonstration by the uncivilized of being completely mad. The practice of politics is the uncivilized enslaving the world to their barbarism. The differences in the natures of the civilized and the uncivilized is evidence that the world is self-sufficient and the purpose of the law should be to protect the individual rights and personal freedoms of the inhabitants of this planet. Politics is about catering to the sadism of the uncivilized, it breeds lawlessness. For the practice of politics to be possible the uncivilized will need to misuse their supernatural powers and senses to create problems and then try to involve everyone in the madness. For politics or demonism or supernaturalism to work there has to be conflicts, it feeds off disaster, insecurity, poverty, charity, the elimination of individual rights and personal freedoms.

According to the guidance of the constitution, its definition of work involves the use of supernatural powers and senses which makes it impossible for the civilized to work because of the lack of supernatural powers and senses.

The practice of politics encourages the deception of contradicting the instructions of the constitution regarding work by the uncivilized pretending to be civilized and misleading the vulnerable including the civilized that the civilized are required to work. The civilized cannot work because we are naturally not able to do that, this does not mean that the civilized are disabled, on the contrary, the civilized were created to govern. The civilized are naturally commissioners of police. The practice of politics by the uncivilized is a conspiracy to persecute the civilized, the vulnerable, contrary to the guidance of the constitution. The deception by the uncivilized pretending to be civilized was not for any good purpose but was part of a collective conspiracy to undermine the constitutional rights of the civilized, in order to alter the civilized nature of the civilized.

The magnitude of the collective deception by the uncivilized aimed at the unlawful persecution of the civilized means that it becomes completely impossible for the civilized not to see the uncivilized collectively as enemies and extremely hazardous.

The constitution instructs that the civilized should trust our surroundings because it anticipates that the civilized should never be exposed to any hostile situation. This inbuilt trust has been compromised by the wickedness of the uncivilized collectively.

The practice of politics encourages the principle of one group of people taking pleasure at the discomfort of another group of people, this breeds violence and instability, and puts the vulnerable including the civilized in serious danger.

Politics is a practice that caters to the barbaric nature of the uncivilized, they use it to compensate for the lack of things to do, their supernatural powers and senses mean that it takes a lot to satisfy them. The different unnecessary government departments are evidence of what it takes to quench the boredom of the uncivilized. Civil servants are capable of performing the duties of government ministers, in government departments that are of any use, given the differences in the natures of the civilized and the uncivilized. The useful government departments do not have to operate in the crazy way they do at present. The constitution encourages less government; the needs of the world should be anticipated and adequately provided for quickly, with little or no effort as a one off. The objective of the constitution is to limit the use of supernatural powers and senses, because of its possible harmful effects.

When the uncivilized misuse their supernatural powers and senses to refuse to acknowledge the constitutional authority of the civilized and our rank in law enforcement as commissioners of police, it means that they intend to continue with their demonic practices, and want to use the law to a limited degree to achieve this objective. When they try to force the civilized into law enforcement into lesser ranks than that recognized by law, it means that they are trying to use the civilized for illegal purposes contrary to the guidance of the constitution, it means that they are trying to use the law (the civilized) to persecute the law (the civilized).

The civilized are isolated from a culture or world that links success to the supernatural, financial security is linked to the supernatural, we are not disabled and we cannot work because we do not have supernatural powers and senses. The governing positions meant for the civilized have been taken over by the uncivilized pretending to be civilized, so in a society that comfort is linked to financial security what are the civilized meant to live on? The uncivilized pretending to be civilized are insisting that every able bodied person should get a job, conspiring to make the civilized work unnecessarily, a serious type or torture or sadism. They are saying while pretending to be civilized that if they can work everyone should look for a job. Their conspiracy to try to undermine the civil rights of the civilized is treason. So when an uncivilized person pretends to be civilized as if doing it for the benefit of the civilized, it is a lie.

The creation of the constitutional living conditions meant for the civilized would reveal that hell is limited to the nature of the uncivilized. This means that the deliberate alterations to the instructions of the constitution with regard to the constitutional living conditions and constitutional authority meant for the civilized is an attempt by the uncivilized to spread around their discomfort.

If there are other civilized people like me without supernatural powers and senses and not the uncivilized pretending to be civilized or altering their uncivilized natures to be civilized, then it will be reasonable to conclude that the civilized and the uncivilized should not be on the same planet. The uncivilized have revealed a serious hatred for the civilized, the magnitude of the persecution of the civilized by the uncivilized means that it is not reasonable to expect the civilized and the uncivilized to live on the same planet.

The constitution is clear in its guidance, without doubt, that the civilized are from birth commissioners of the metropolitan police force, given the differences in the natures of the civilized and uncivilized. Any direct or indirect obstruction of the official confirmation of this with regard to the rights and privileges, salary of this office, is an act of terrorism by the uncivilized. It is stipulated in the constitution that the uncivilized are the ones to make sure that the civilized are confirmed immediately, officially as commissioners of police with the rights and privileges. This serves to educate and protect the civilized from the intrusive abusive behaviours of the uncivilized.

The same way the fictional character Data in the science fiction drama series Star Trek the next generation has been programmed with in information, the civilized have been programmed because of our civil nature to identify the rules or laws, which make us the civilized rulers. The civilized are guided by our natural instincts; these good peaceful instincts help guide our decision making. It also helps if our trusting nature is not abused by the uncivilized by the education of the civilized being compromised with misleading information and misleading practices or behaviours.

The civilized cannot move about freely because the world has been deliberately made unsafe for the civilized by the uncivilized, contrary to the guidance of the constitution. The differences in the civilized and the uncivilized mean that the instructions of the constitution have to be implemented for it to be safe for the civilized to move about freely. The uncivilized have been and continue to misuse their supernatural powers and senses to use the law (the civilized) for illegal purposes, this means that the civilized (the law) will have to be made slaves or prisoners for these illegal purposes. The civilized are deliberately made to move about as open targets for the uncivilized to cater to their sadistic nature. Without the constitutional authority or civil powers meant for the civilized, the civilized have been illegally rendered disabled for the barbarism of the uncivilized.

The constitution is quite clear on the misuse of supernatural powers and senses in circumstances that require the civilized to kill insects, when our homes are deliberately infested with insects, the guidance is in the situation in the Christian teachings, in Egypt when Moses wanted to get Pharaoh to let the Israelites leave Egypt when the Israelites were enslaved by the Egyptians, when Moses with supernatural powers was able to infest the whole of Egypt with locust. The lesson really is for the uncivilized not to delude themselves into believing that they can blame the civilized for what they are directly or indirectly responsible for, regardless of appearances.

The uncivilized should not delude themselves into believing that they can misuse their supernatural powers and senses to create problems for the civilized as if trying to test us. The civilized are naturally good; the source of any problem will be amongst the uncivilized.

The civilized are pawns in the red and blue games of the uncivilized. Reds is in reference to red devils and blue is meant to be angels. From their definition of reds, the uncivilized participating in these games whether they refer to themselves as reds or blues are collectively reds meaning red devils. Both the uncivilized referring to themselves as reds or those referring to themselves as blues have both conspired to compromise the development and education of the civilized in order to use the civilized(gods) as pawns in their game of death.

The civilized are not telepaths, we do not have supernatural powers and senses, things have to be explained to us properly and not in riddles or problems to solve.

The military, the police forces use uniforms to signify the uniformity of purpose to maintain order (civility). The symbol the star sign used to acknowledge the most senior ranks in the military is a representation of the civilized nature of the civilized. These are acknowledgements of the civilized as commissioners of police. The star sign is a representation of the civilized because of the differences in the natures of the civilized and the uncivilized, the enhanced sense of sight of the uncivilized means that they watch the civilized and the civilized are naturally good harmless(peaceful). The uncivilized are prepared to wear the symbol of the civilized as something that gives them respect and dignity or honour and use these privileges to persecute the civilized.

The right to privacy is a civil right that is essential because of the supernatural senses of the uncivilized, and its intrusive, harmful nature.

According to the guidance of the constitution, which is the Christian principles, civil rights, the purpose of the law is to prevent the misuse of supernatural powers and senses to undermine the constitutional authority of the civilized. It is also meant to prevent the misuse of supernatural powers and senses to undermine the constitutional living conditions of the civilized. The constitution confirms that the problem the world has been experiencing is as a direct result of the constitutional authority of Adam being compromised, in the Garden of Eden. All the positive technological advancements at present are still too primitive to meet the requirements for the constitutional living conditions for the civilized outlined in the Garden of Eden in the Christian teachings. The constitution does not tolerate any direct or indirect, intentional or unintentional misuse of supernatural powers and senses to undermine or compromise the constitutional authority of the civilized, by the uncivilized.

Once it became clear that I had completely rejected the uncivilized when they decided to reveal the existence of the differences in their uncivilized natures and my civilized nature, I was subjected to constant attacks by the uncivilized, they were illegally communicating to me supernaturally, my thoughts were being interfered with, there were strange body movements that I could not control, my dreams were and continue to be interfered with, and my body was illegally altered by the uncivilized. They are spiteful, vindictive; it makes no difference to them that the civilized are naturally incapable of committing crimes or sinning. They believe what they want to, in order to justify the illegal supernatural attacks on the civilized.

The uncivilized have collectively conspired to make the civilized believe that to have access to our civil rights which is an automatic entitlement because of our civil nature, we have to become supernatural, we have to lose our civil rights in order to get our civil rights, contrary to the guidance of the constitution. In order to effect this deception they are unlawfully delaying the complete implementation of the instructions of the constitution, including the official confirmation of the civilized as commissioners of the metropolitan police force.

They have unlawfully conspired in order to effect the deception, to make the civilized believe that we have to worship the uncivilized to have access to our civil rights. This is evidenced by the mosques, synagogues, and churches where the civilized are made to illegally worship the uncivilized or the supernatural, contrary to the guidance of the constitution. With this in mind, it is reasonable to conclude that the uncivilized will continue to misuse their supernatural powers and senses to put the civilized in compromising situations to discredit the civilized because of their continuous efforts to try to undermine the constitutional authority of the civilized.

The constitution is in place to prevent the strong (the uncivilized) from dominating the weak (the civilized) by misusing their supernatural powers and senses.

And I also believe that the constitution is trying to educate the supernatural that real strength is to aspire to the characteristics or qualities of the civilized nature.

Direct or indirect contact with the civilized is not allowed unless in accordance with the guidance of constitution, the civilized must first be confirmed as rulers of the uncivilized officially; this requirement is as a consequence of the abusive nature of the uncivilized. An uncivilized person pretending to be civilized does not fulfil this requirement. The uncivilized have refused to obey the instructions of the constitution because they wrongly believe that they are superior to the civilized. So they will do everything possible to avoid the sacred instructions of the constitution, including creating hell on earth. Everything in this sacred world confirms that they cannot avoid the complete implementation of the instructions of the constitution. According to the guidance of the constitution, regardless of how long life is meant to be, the constitutional authority and constitutional living conditions of the civilized should be effected immediately. According to the guidance of the constitution life is meant to go on indefinitely. There is the risk that because life is meant to go on indefinitely, the instructions of the constitution meant to be implemented immediately will be put off, taken for granted. These instructions are to be effected immediately; they are part of living regardless of how long life is meant to go on for.

The uncivilized misuse their supernatural powers and senses to plan the lives of the civilized as if we are inanimate objects or animals they are feeding for their consumption at a later date, or slaves or prisoners. So I must conclude in my capacity as a commissioner of police that unless the instructions of the constitution are implemented completely, I have no choice but to declare that the uncivilized collectively are enemies of the state, world and universe, and are not welcomed in the dominion of the civilized.

Unlike the criminal activity of politics, the civilized do not need the approval of the public to be confirmed as commissioners of police, the constitution has already established the moral superiority of the civilized.

The uncivilized have a problem or cannot handle life the way it was originally intended, the natural life span being indefinite and the approved constitutional living conditions. According to the guidance of the constitution, it is the only way life works regardless of one's views or opinions. If they cannot handle it, why create life, they are the only ones capable of creating life. The civilized are law enforcement officers or rulers, we make sure that the law is identified, interpreted and applied correctly once life is created. In the same way that parents are not allowed to abuse their children with the illegal laws that still indirectly permit abuses in other ways, but the principle is the same. The constitution does not permit the misuse of supernatural powers and senses by the uncivilized to harm the vulnerable, the civilized or to breach the peace in a civilized society. It appears that my computer is becoming temperamental; its grammar and spell check is not working properly because of illegal supernatural interference. I will take this as a compliment, because the truth is affecting the wicked to the extent that they want to undermine my efforts.

When the uncivilized start harming the civilized mentally or physically with their supernatural powers and senses under the guise of punishment implying that the civilized are doing something wrong in the context of a crime or a sin, it is an unprovoked attacked on the civilized aimed at undermining the constitutional authority of the civilized. The constitution has already predetermined that the civilized are incapable of wrongdoing (sinning or committing crimes).

The civilized do not like any uncivilized person that much to tolerate or permit the misuse of supernatural powers and senses to cause the civilized mental or physical injury, the misuse of supernatural powers and senses is an extremely serious matter. If an uncivilized person is not aware of the seriousness of the misuse of supernatural powers and senses, that person is mad, regardless of how minor they think the infringement is. Appearances can be deceptive, the civilized do not react to hostile situations the same way an uncivilized person will, but the rejection of the hostile act by the civilized is more effective, although it might appear subtle compared to the ineffective approach of the uncivilized. The constitution's screening of the uncivilized for security purposes regarding the protection of the civilized is infallible, regardless of appearances.

When the uncivilized that are aspiring to become real police officers , are able to identify the constitution's definition of real crimes, and what is involved in solving crimes and deterring and preventing crimes, who are entitled to real civil rights, then it will become clear to them that the civilized are the commissioners of the metropolitan police force.

The differences are so massive that to avoid the civilized having to live our lives feeling constantly threatened, there was no margin for error with the installation of the civil powers of the civilized, to expose the civilized to the misuse of supernatural powers and senses without the protection of our civil powers is an abomination. The uncivilized do not quite comprehend the magnitude of this breach of trust and security. They have sown the seeds of doubt or mistrust which will never be recovered. They still persist because of their collective sadism to initiate unwanted contact with the civilized without the protection of the civil powers of the civilized.

Civil powers are the official confirmation of the civilized as commissioners of the metropolitan police force, with the real rights and privileges. It is not a request, it is a constitutional instruction.

2. PUNISHMENT

How do you deter those with superhuman strengths from misusing their supernatural powers and senses to harm the vulnerable, the civilized mentally or physically, to breach the peace in a civilized society? The conventional method of punishment in the world, the criminal justice system, encourages criminal behaviour rather than deters criminal behaviour given the supernatural powers and senses of the uncivilized. According to the guidance of the constitution the uncivilized are the only ones capable of committing crimes because of their supernatural powers and senses.

Given the circumstances involving the continuous existence of the creator and Adam in the Garden of Eden in the Christian teachings, there is a model of the civilized and the uncivilized coexisting peacefully. This should suggest that there should be a possibility of deterring the misuse of supernatural powers and senses with sensible punishments that would have the effect of deterring those with superhuman strengths from committing crimes in the future. The creation of hell will suggest that it has already been predetermined to be the only way to deter those with superhuman strengths because of their supernatural powers and senses from committing crimes. The uncivilized collectively have not yet disproved this conclusion. I am sure the creator will want to be proved wrong with regard to this type of punishment.

The uncivilized should be aware that everything needs a degree of order. The world cannot exist without order. The purpose of punishment and rehabilitation should be for the uncivilized to experience life without order. This is the reasoning behind the creation of hell. Hell is a punishment designed to go on forever. According to the guidance of the constitution the punishment created for the uncivilized is based on an extreme type of intolerable torture that is meant to go on indefinitely which reflects the constitution's disapproval of the way the uncivilized misuse their supernatural powers and senses to plan the lives of the civilized. When the uncivilized misuse their supernatural powers and senses to harm the civilized mentally or physically they are automatically enemies of the state and fugitives from real justice regardless of appearances.

The current prison system created by the uncivilized serves as a reward for criminal behaviour given the superhuman strengths associated with the supernatural powers and senses of the uncivilized. It only deters the civilized that the constitution confirms are incapable of committing crimes because of the lack of supernatural powers and senses.

According to the guidance of the constitution, the uncivilized or the creator and the civilized or the ruler were able to sustain a peaceful relationship for a period before one was disobedient. The test for the uncivilized aspiring to become real police officers is to identify the source of the disobedient or unlawful behaviour that led to the end of the peaceful relationship between the ruler and the creator. I am in no way suggesting child abuse. But culpability needs to be established in order to properly establish and maintain law and order taking into account that Adam never had supernatural powers and senses that triggered a chain of events that led to the alteration of his civil nature that led to Adam being overthrown from his position as the legitimate ruler.

It is reasonable to conclude that since the alteration or shift in the balance of power between the civilized and the uncivilized resulting from the conspiracy in the Garden of Eden, the world is still suffering and has not recovered from that, it has gradually evolved from paradise to hell on earth.

This is why the constitution does not tolerate and cannot afford to tolerate any circumstances involving the uncivilized trying to undermine the constitutional authority of the civilized.

When establishing culpability of a criminal offence you do not choose the vulnerable or victim as the offender because it is easier or you will not encounter any problems from unlawfully punishing the person that will offer less resistance. The current unlawful practice is to blame the vulnerable, the civilized, rather than the uncivilized, because the civilized will offer no resistance because of the lack of supernatural powers and senses to being framed for crimes we are incapable of committing.

Once I became aware of the differences in the nature of the uncivilized and my civil nature that they were hiding, I was very surprised that given the possibilities there really should be nothing to fight or quarrel over. The differences in the civilized and the uncivilized were meant to complement each other. The only problem I could establish immediately is the need for the uncivilized to satisfy their barbaric urges associated with their supernatural instincts. They have the ability to draw out conflict from the jaws of peace because of their uncivilized instincts. The alarming thing is that they believe that their destructive barbarisms are jokes and games. The uncivilized speak a completely different language from the civilized, they comprehend things differently too.

The problems associated with the misuse of supernatural powers and senses are excessive that have destabilized the peace and security in the world required to sustain or preserve life. Unless there are adequate measures in place to prevent or deter the uncivilized from misusing their supernatural powers and senses to harm the vulnerable, the civilized and to breach the peace in the world, it becomes impossible to sustain or preserve life.

According to the guidance of the constitution, given the supernatural powers and senses of the uncivilized, death could be used as a way to escape real punishment.

According to the guidance of the constitution, regarding policing and punishment, the creator or the supernatural was responsible for the policing and punishment of the uncivilized Adam, in order to protect the integrity of the civilized or civilized society the Garden of Eden.

The Garden of Eden by its nature commissioned the creator to protect it from unlawful behaviour.

3. AUTHOR'S NOTES

This is my sixth non-fiction book about the law. It is about what I believe to be the correct identification, interpretation and application of the constitution of the planet. It is a no nonsense approach to law enforcement. The book reveals that the uncivilized, those with supernatural powers and senses represent a constant threat to the peace and security of this planet and adequate measures need to be put in place to deter or prevent the misuse of their supernatural powers and senses to harm the civilized, those without supernatural powers and senses, the vulnerable, and to breach the peace in a civilized society. The current problems in the world are as a consequence of the uncivilized always getting emotional without the benefit of intellect. They allow themselves to be guided by their supernatural instincts or emotions and as a consequence are undermining law and order by interfering with the constitutional rights of the peace makers the civilized. The emotions or instincts of the uncivilized have made them try to compete with the civilized that are by nature law enforcement officers, they are trying to undermine the peace and security of this planet.

I have had to give up my interests or hobbies because the uncivilized have misused their supernatural powers and senses to make them unsafe and unhealthy for misguided purposes.

4. AUTHOR'S BIOGRAPHY

My name is Lord Loveday Ememe. I am a graduate of an Anglican seminary school. I graduated from the University of East London with a law degree. I am of a civilized nature; I have no supernatural powers and senses.

Bibliography

The Bible.